The Way of the Cross

**Illustrations and Meditations By:
Gail Artola**

The Way of the Cross

Copyright © 2005 by Gail Artola

The Way of the Cross
by Gail Artola

Printed in the United States of America

ISBN 1-59781-640-X

All rights reserved solely by the author. The author guarantees all contents are original and do not infringe upon the legal rights of any other person or work. No part of this book may be reproduced in any form without the permission of the author. The views expressed in this book are not necessarily those of the publisher.

www.xulonpress.com

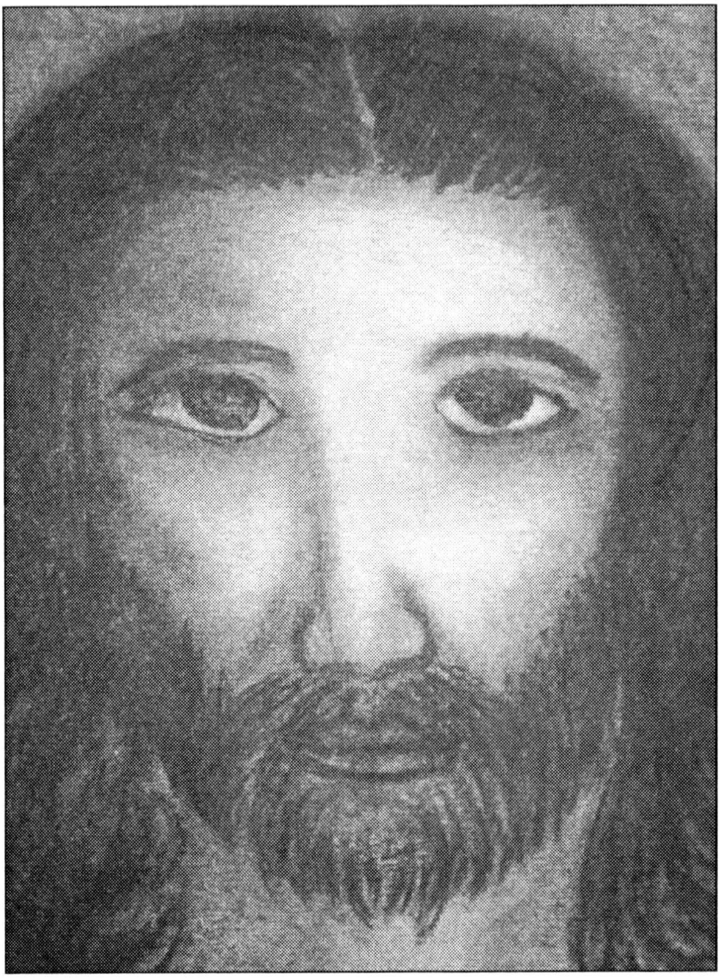

INTRODUCTION

Welcome to the Stations of the Cross
Here you will see what Jesus went through
On this journey from shadows to darkness
You will find that this is all about you

And so each chapter is written
That you may be made aware
Of all that Jesus had done for you
But the Way of the Cross does not end there

First you will see the Cross of Jesus
The next part is the crosses we make
That we have made for ourselves and others
By our sins errors and mistakes

Next you will see the crosses you take
Crosses that you yourself have known
Life deals crosses but in the end you'll see
You do not carry these crosses alone

† † † † † † † † † † † † † † † † † † † †

Here I will show you the Way of the Cross
This Cross will show you the way to Me
Take my hand, for you are not alone
Together let us begin this journey

I
SHADOWS

JESUS IS CONDEMNED TO DEATH

The angry condemning fingers
Point at the innocent man
No one ever says why
But everyone understands

Just because it is unanimous
Doesn't mean it is right
When there is a life in the balance
Fading in the shadows of the darkest night

With no protest from the accused
And a crowd shouting "Crucify"
Pilate gave them what they wanted
And condemned this man to die

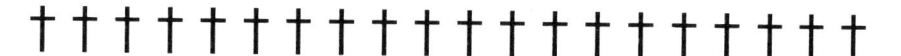

† † † † † † † † † † † † † † † † † † † †

For when you followed the crowd
And when you pointed the blame
For the innocent blood on your hands
For your pride made out of another's shame

For when you were innocent
And had taken the fall
For when you stood all alone
And no one answered your call

For when your life didn't matter
For when you were betrayed
For when you gave all you had
And never got repaid

I am here in this place
Because of my love for you
I am standing in these shadows
And suffering all you go through

II
AGONY

JESUS TAKES HIS CROSS

His eyes are searching for his friends
A condemning crowd is all He sees
The soldiers drag Jesus away
And push Him down onto His knees

They grab His wrists and extend His arms
Onto His shoulders they place the beam
No one saw the sins it contained
Nor the souls it would redeem

For these souls His passion burned
Gathering strength through His agony
He stands up and begins to walk
This excursion to Calvary

† † † † † † † † † † † † † † † † † † † †

For when you had laid a burden
Upon a brother's back
For when you took it upon yourself
To violate, punish and attack

For when you were excluded
And you had been pushed down
For when you searched for help
And no friends were around

For when you obediently taken
The cross that was given to you
For when the road ahead is long
And you attempted to follow through

I am here in this place
Because of my love for you
I am opening my arms to agony
And suffering all you go through

III
TEARS

JESUS FALLS THE FIRST TIME

Imagine every sin ever committed
The sins of you and of I and of all
It breaks His heart and brings tears to His eyes
And are heavy enough to make God fall

There is a lamb just out of His reach
It is a reminder of who he is
He's the sacrifice of the Father
And this cross makes us His

It also reminds Him He's a Shepherd
And we are His wandering lost sheep
It motivates Him to continue on
Because He has a promise to keep

† † † † † † † † † † † † † † † † † † †

For all the sins you committed
Adding to the weight of My Cross
For all the confessions never made
The pieces of your soul forever lost

For the times you laid broken
For when you had a desperate need
For when you picked up your cross again
And continued to follow lead

For when you find the courage
To pick yourself up and stand
For when you start over again
I offer you my hand

I am here in this place
Because of my love for you
I am crying these tears of falling
And suffering all you go through

IV
DESPAIR

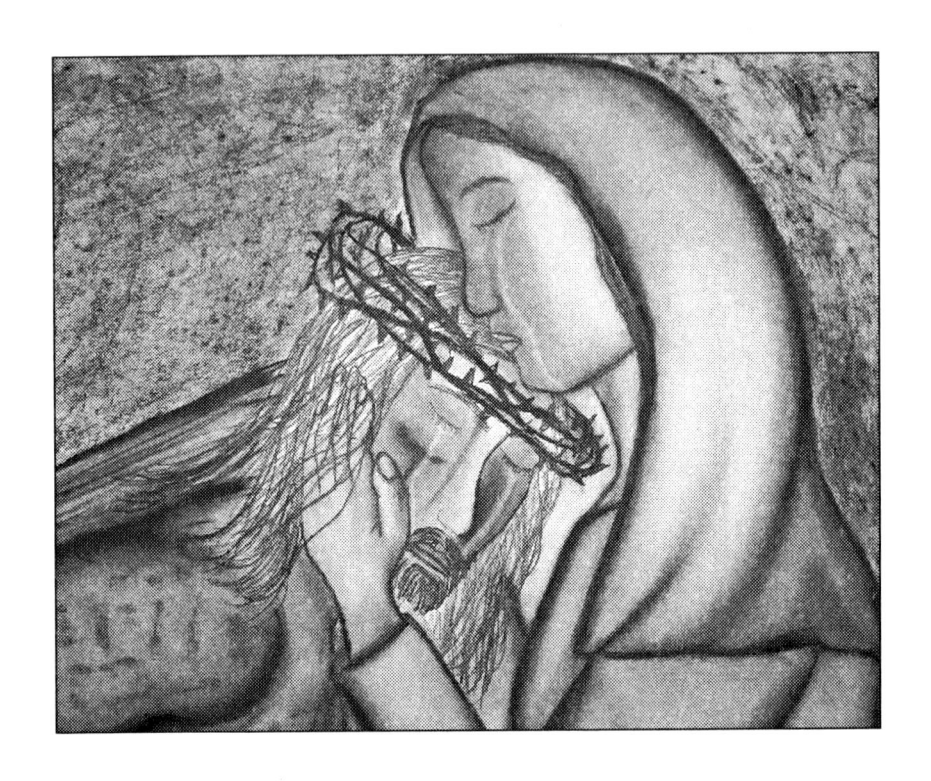

JESUS MEETS HIS AFFLICTED MOTHER

When He sees her He makes a wish
That His blood and pain He could cover
That the cursing crowd could be silenced
In the presence of His mother

But He can't change this shameful scene
Bows down to hide the pain on His face
He knows that a sword is piercing her heart
And that she is praying to take His place

She embraces Him with one last kiss
He doesn't have to hide or pretend
He offers her His own despair
She returns faithfulness to the end

✝ ✝ ✝ ✝ ✝ ✝ ✝ ✝ ✝ ✝ ✝ ✝ ✝ ✝ ✝ ✝ ✝ ✝ ✝ ✝

For when failure destroys your courage
And you no longer have the strength to care
For when you were embarrassed
And your painful secrets you would not share

For when you had the compassion
To join in someone else's pain
And still you opened your heart
Knowing your heart will be slain

For when you watched a loved one
In illness, heartache and strife
For when you prayed the desperate prayer
Trading places and offering your life

I am here in this place
Because of my love for you
I am weak in your presence
And suffering all you go through

V
WHISPERS

SIMON OF CYRENE HELPS JESUS

Death in the streets is not enough
They want to see Jesus crucified
So they grab a bystander to help
So the torture they planned is not denied

Unwilling to fulfill the role
Casted by strangers to play the part
But Simon changed when he looked in His eyes
And felt the beat of His Sacred Heart

Jesus whispers to His beloved
The intimacy filled his soul's need
And so he holds Jesus closer
Feeling His thorns, together they bleed

✝✝✝✝✝✝✝✝✝✝✝✝✝✝✝✝✝✝✝✝

For when you would not get involved
For when you refused when you were asked
For when you are selfish with your time
And when you ignored a simple task

For when you were the helpful stranger
The angel without wings
For when you treated the least among you
Like the noblest of kings

For the first time you spoke into the wind
Hoping I would respond somehow
For all the ways I've spoken to you since
For the relationship we have now

I am here in this place
Because of my love for you
I am entering into your soul
And suffering all you go through

VI
LABYRINTHS

VERONICA WIPES THE FACE OF JESUS

The hearts of the crowd grow darker
Like vicious hounds they bark and bite
Who add dark to darkness with hatred
But in the dark you can see starlight

A star was the first to tell the world
Telling of Jesus to all who gaze
Giving hope to the labyrinths of our souls
Leading to Jesus in the black maze

Veronica saw the star of Heaven
Recognized the Savior and wiped His face
She in turn was a star to Jesus
He left her His image, a special grace

✝✝✝✝✝✝✝✝✝✝✝✝✝✝✝✝✝✝✝

For when the darkness was there
And you helped the darkness to grow
For when the pain of a person
Became an entertaining show

For when you reached to the dimmest light
Inside a darkness so great
For when you refused to bow
And resisted evil and hate

For when you gave compassionately
Without ever counting the cost
For when you stood up for Jesus
The Redeemer of the lost

I am here in this place
Because of my love for you
I am wandering the darkened labyrinths
And suffering all you go through

VII
ALONE

JESUS FALLS A SECOND TIME

Mary, Simon and Veronica
Offer Jesus strength for the journey
But He falls down beyond their reach
Alone He goes where they cannot be

He slips away under the surface
Engulfed in the ocean of despair
Mercy lies in the arms of death
So He asks for death in a prayer

But His request for death is denied
Instead God grants Him a vision of all
Of our souls suffering in damnation
Out of love He gets up from the fall

† † † † † † † † † † † † † † † † † † † †

For when you made the God of hope distant
And made death and despair a close friend
For when agony or self-hatred
Leaves you begging for your life to end

For when you find yourself on the path
Of a journey lonely, dark and far
This is the road of your soul's destiny
That makes you who you are

For when you heart is bleeding
From the wounds that cut inside
For the scars that never heal
But surely know how to hide

I am here in this place
Because of my love for you
I am traveling this path alone
And suffering all you go through

VIII
FEAR

JESUS MEETS THE WOMEN OF JERUSALEM

The women of Jerusalem prayed
That this Savior's life God would spare
But God did not fulfill their request
No miracles, just unanswered prayer

Their hearts were overcome with fear
The fear replaces the faith that once dwelt there
Why continue to believe in Him
When it seems God Himself does not care?

Jesus redirected their tears
"Weep for your children, not for me"
When the love in His eyes met with theirs
They trusted in what is to be

† † † † † † † † † † † † † † † † † † †

For the sleepless nights strained by worry
For when you did not trust and let go
For when you were not calm and patient
Demanding the answers you want to know

For when your courtship with hope
Ended in another lonely night
For when things seemed impossible
And there is no salvation in sight

For when fear has claimed you life
And your soul is lying in the dust
For when my promises seemed broken
And still in me you placed you trust

I am here in this place
Because of my love for you
I am fearing for your soul
And suffering all you go through

IX
IRONY

JESUS FALLS A THIRD TIME

Love is hated, Healer is suffering
Life is dying, Strength becomes weak
The Deliverer is handed over
The Teacher, the Rabbi can hardly speak

The Creator is made broken
The Way becomes confused and lost
The Breath of life is breathless
The Truth and Freedom has become the cost

Son of Heaven facing demons of hell
Restorer damaged, Fulfillment bleeding
The irony of Jesus' death
God falls and is desperately needing

† †

For when you were the relative estranged
And the friend who became enemy
For when the lover of your soul
Cried tears for you in Gethsemane

For old familiar tears cried again
Revisited agony in your soul
For ghosts from the past that haunt your life
Preventing you from becoming whole

For the terrors covered by painted smiles
For dead end roads and unheard screams
For how you started and what you became
For high hopes shattered and broken dreams

I am here in this place
Because of my love for you
I am losing all that I am
And suffering all you go through

X
DESECRATED

JESUS IS STRIPPED OF HIS CLOTHES

At Golgotha, the Place of the Skull
The cross is taken off His shoulder
The mocking words continue to burn
As the soldiers grow ever colder

Then the sound of tearing cloth
Quiets the crowd as it cuts the air
Clothed in nothing but His own blood
Feeling the weight of the crowd's stare

Stripped of dignity, covered in shame
Naked, exposed and invaded
An embarrassing bow, eyes turned down
For who will love the desecrated?

† † † † † † † † † † † † † † † † † † † †

For gossip and slander of words
For the thrill and power of an attack
For all that you have taken away
That you could never give back

For the child neglected and abused
Those wounds that never completely heal
For the damaged heart, the distorted soul
Left believing true love is not real

For the victims silenced by fear
Pretending it never happened at all
For when you vowed to trust no one
And around your heart built a wall

I am here in this place
Because of my love for you
I am shamefully desecrated
And suffering all you go through

XI
PAIN

JESUS IS NAILED TO THE CROSS

The executioners begin their work
A job they do well in and take pride
Heroes carrying out the law
Acceptable murderers on our side

Jesus tries to look into their eyes
But never once do they look back
For what can this insane preacher offer
To those who never need or never lack?

As they press the nail into His skin
Clenching His teeth, He tries to stay silent
He watches as the hammer comes swinging down
He screams out from a pain so violent

† † † † † † † † † † † † † † † † † † † †

For when you are lured by power
By promising leaders we glamorize
For when you sell your soul to conform
For when you believe the selfish lies

For the blood spilled in the battle
For the devastation of war
For when victims become a statistic
And the world's not the same anymore

For the pain that burns right through your soul
The tears you cry, the anguished screams
The still and hollow numbness that follows
For the shattered future and lost dreams

I am here in this place
Because of my love for you
I am screaming in pain
And suffering all you go through

XII
DEATH

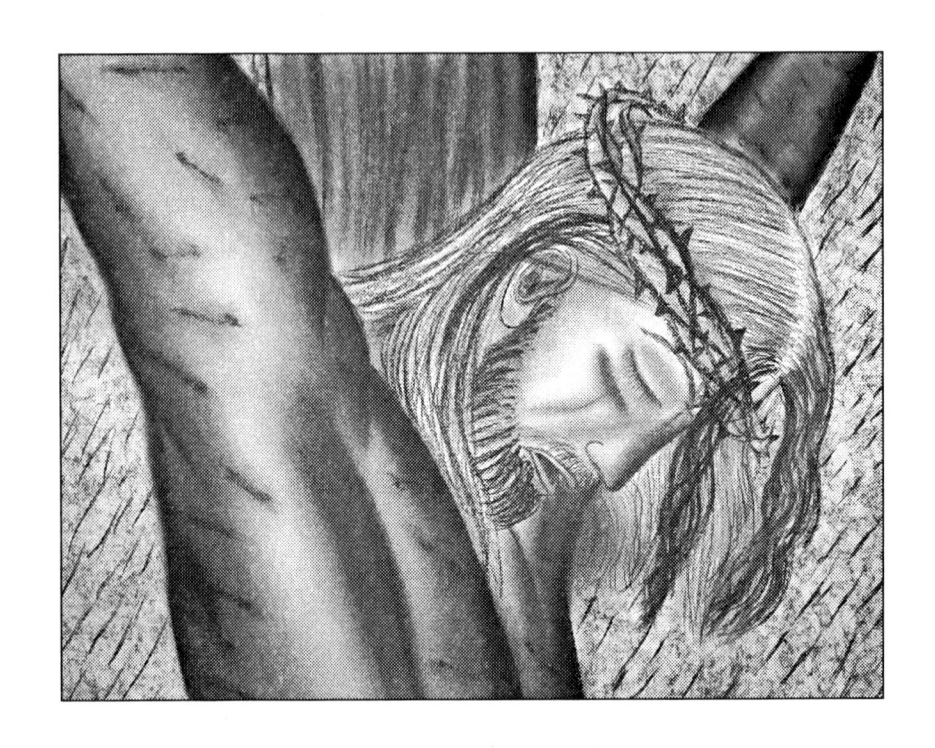

JESUS DIES ON THE CROSS

Upon the Cross He offers forgiveness
To a repented sinner - paradise
Lastly Jesus gives away His mother
Giving all, He becomes the sacrifice

Asks, "Oh God why have you abandoned me"
Then prays the prayers of a man near death
It is all over now, take My soul
Thirsting, bleeding, He breathes His last breath

Never before or since in history
Can these thoughts be uttered or words be said
And dare we speak this truth aloud
That this is our God and our God is dead

† † † † † † † † † † † † † † † † † † † †

For how easily you can forget
And even less do you care
That Jesus gave His life for you
And still you doubt His love is there

For every life must end in death
A fate that cannot be debated
For those final moments of your life
When joys and regrets are contemplated

For the addictions and vices
The relentless demons you let inside
For the hour of your own death
For the God from whom you cannot hide

I am here in this place
Because of my love for you
I am sacrificing all that I am
And suffering all you go through

XIII
SORROW

THE BODY OF JESUS IS TAKEN DOWN

With a sword the heart of Jesus is pierced
Blood and water flow from His side
Surely this is the Son of God
Who like a criminal we crucified

God who dwells in the temple's core
Tears the curtain as He leaves
For we have killed His beloved Son
Immense are the sorrows when God grieves

Creation mourns and the angels cry
Their tears are found in the pouring rain
His body is given to His mother
She holds her lifeless Son, crying in pain

✝✝✝✝✝✝✝✝✝✝✝✝✝✝✝✝✝✝

For the many times you hurt God
And still expect Him to always be there
Telling Him you deserve more than you got
Complaining that what He deals is unfair

For when you map out your plans in life
With bows to take and achievements to earn
For when you loose all that you live for
When the path of life takes a sudden turn

For when you mourn and suffer a loss
The loved one there is abruptly gone
The pain of grieving that leaves you empty
Wondering how you will ever go on

I am here in this place
Because of my love for you
I am becoming hopeless sorrow
And suffering all you go through

XIV
DARKNESS

JESUS IS LAID IN THE TOMB

Mary pondered these things in her heart
As she has since Jesus was in her womb
The secrets she keeps, the life she has known
She now buries with her Son in the tomb

Jesus bears more than this Cross
His battle continues beyond the grave
He descends to face the demons of hell
Where there are more souls He must save

Darkness holds the intimacy of God
Where no eyes can see but the truth is said
For in the dark is where your life began
In the darkness Jesus rose from the dead

† † † † † † † † † † † † † † † † † † † †

For when you buried your own soul
And put to death the light inside
For when you find evil intriguing
For all the truths you have denied

For the secrets that shout in the dark
And the dreams that dance and play in the night
For all your heart's deepest desires
That you pray will someday take to flight

For when you were afraid of the dark
For when you were lost and could not see
For when you take up your cross and follow
I offer my life to set you free

I am here in this place
Because of my love for you
I am coming to you in the darkness
And suffering all you go through

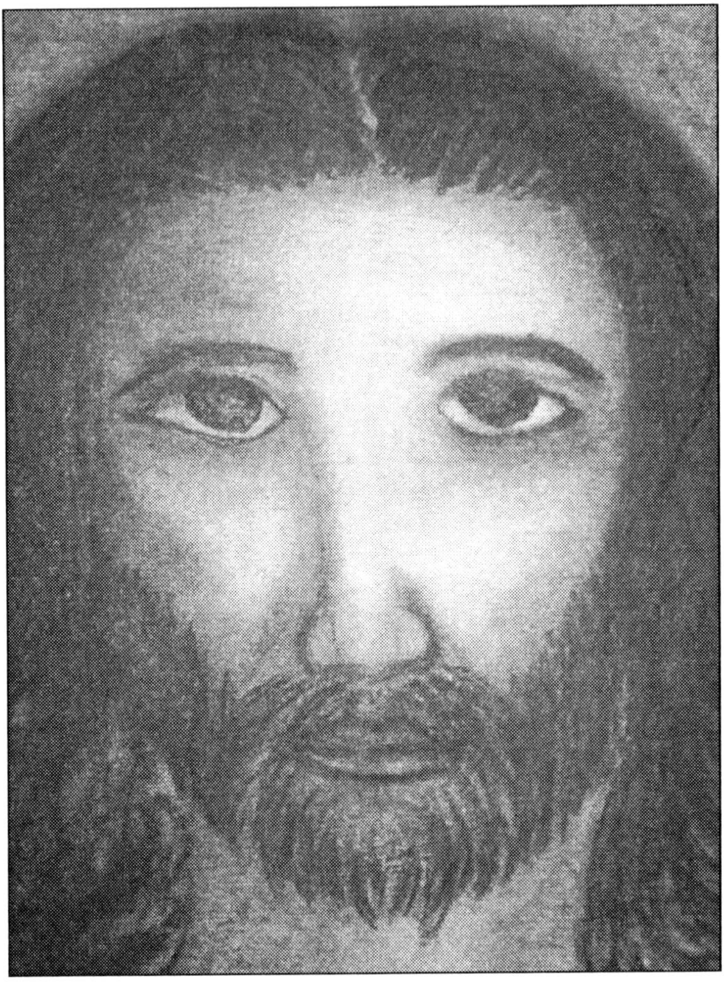

Conclusion

In the stillness of the dark
And in the silence of the night
We learn that although hope will struggle
It will never give up on the fight

On this journey you have taken
You experienced the Cross Jesus bore
He loves you and died for you
To open up wide Heaven's door

On this journey Jesus has taken
He experienced the life you have known
He loves you and lived for you
So you would never have to walk alone

Salvation is real and within reach
No matter what kind of life you have led
Remember every saint has a past
And every sinner has a future ahead

† † † † † † † † † † † † † † † † † † †

Here I have shown you the Way of the Cross
This Cross has shown you the way to Me
Take Me now into your heart and soul
And invite Me on your life journey

Printed in the United States
44635LVS00007B